Scariest Places
on
Earth

THE DEAD SEA

By Therese Shea

Gareth Stevens
PUBLISHING

Please visit our website, www.garethstevens.com. For a free color catalog of all our high-quality books, call toll free 1-800-542-2595 or fax 1-877-542-2596.

Library of Congress Cataloging-in-Publication Data

Shea, Therese.
The Dead Sea / by Therese Shea.
 p. cm. — (Scariest places on Earth)
Includes index.
ISBN 978-1-4824-1167-6 (pbk.)
ISBN 978-1-4824-1168-3 (6-pack)
ISBN 978-1-4824-1166-9 (library binding)
1. Dead Sea (Israel and Jordan) — Juvenile literature. I. Shea, Therese. II. Title.
DS110.D38 S54 2014
956.94—d23

First Edition

Published in 2015 by
Gareth Stevens Publishing
111 East 14th Street, Suite 349
New York, NY 10003

Copyright © 2015 Gareth Stevens Publishing

Designer: Katelyn E. Reynolds
Editor: Therese Shea

Photo credits: Cover, p. 1 Dmytro Tokar/E+/Getty Images; cover, pp. 1–24 (background texture) Eky Studio/Shutterstock.com; cover, pp. 1–24 (creepy design elements) Dmitry Natashin/Shutterstock.com; pp. 5 (inset), 13 Noam Armonn/Shutterstock.com; p. 5 (main) Planet Observer/Universal Images Group/Getty Images; p. 7 Eldad Carin/Shutterstock.com; p. 9 Jason Jones Travel Photography/Flickr/Getty Images; p. 11 Nickolay Vinokurov/Shutterstock.com; p. 15 Jonathan Nackstrand/AFP/Getty Images; p. 16 kojik/Shutterstock.com; p. 17 (inset) Warren Price Photography/Shutterstock.com; p. 17 (main) Stocktrek Images/Getty Images; p. 19 Spencer Platt/Getty Images.

Printed in the United States of America

CPSIA compliance information: Batch #CS15GS: For further information contact Gareth Stevens, New York, New York at 1-800-542-2595.

CONTENTS

Words in the glossary appear in **bold** type the first time they are used in the text.

KILLER WATERS?

Imagine a place where no plants and animals live. If they tried to live there, they'd die. That's a pretty scary idea, isn't it? There's a place like that on Earth. It's called the Dead Sea. It's located between the countries of Israel and Jordan in the **Middle East**. The West Bank territory borders its northwestern shores.

The Dead Sea gets many visitors each year. However, if you visit this famous place, there are reasons to be careful. Don't bother to pack your fishing pole. You won't catch any fish while you're there!

Syria

West Bank

Mediterranean
Sea

Dead Sea

Gaza Strip

Israel

Jordan

Egypt

Despite its scary name, there are a lot
of fun facts about the Dead Sea.

SALTY, SALTY WATER

Land animals and people won't die if they step into the Dead Sea. But fish, plants, and other **aquatic** creatures don't stand a chance. That's because the water is very different from other bodies of water. It's like poison to aquatic life!

The Dead Sea is very salty, much more so than any ocean waters. It contains between 28 and 35 percent **saline**. Is that a lot? That's 10 times saltier than most ocean water! The Dead Sea is also called the Salt Sea.

FRIGHTENING OR FUN?

The Dead Sea's name has been traced back to between 323 BC and 30 BC. That means people have known about its deadly qualities for a very long time.

Here's another tricky fact about the Dead Sea: It's actually a lake! A lake is a large inland body of slowly moving or standing water.

HOLD THE SALT

The salt that's found in the Dead Sea isn't the same kind of salt that you sprinkle on your popcorn. The Dead Sea contains 35 kinds of **mineral** salts. These include calcium, iodine, and magnesium.

Evaporation is the reason there's so much salt in the Dead Sea. In summer, that area of the Middle East can be as hot as 118°F (48°C). Water flowing into the Dead Sea evaporates quickly. The mineral salts in the water get left behind.

The Jordan River is one of the Dead Sea's main **tributaries**. Though the river is freshwater, it contains minerals that resulted in the salty nature of the Dead Sea.

9

BACTERIA AT THE BOTTOM

For a long time, scientists believed nothing could live in the Dead Sea. However, in recent years, scientists have found **bacteria** in craters at the lake's bottom. These tiny life-forms can live there because some freshwater is leaking into the lake from underground springs.

It's hard to study the Dead Sea bacteria because the salty water is always pushing divers to the surface! Scientists do know that the bacteria have found a way to stay alive even when the water around them gets saltier.

FRIGHTENING OR FUN?

Another reason it's hard for divers to explore the Dead Sea is that the salty water can burn their eyes if they aren't careful!

The Dead Sea is more than 1,360 feet (415 m) below sea level. Its shores are the lowest dry point on Earth!

11

DISAPPEARING!

The Dead Sea is 50 miles (80 km) long and 11 miles (18 km) across at its widest point. However, it's shrinking every year. People's use of the Jordan River is a major reason for this.

Governments and businesses are changing the path of, or diverting, the river's water so they can have freshwater for businesses, farms, and personal use. That means less water is ending up in the Dead Sea. Meanwhile, the water of the Dead Sea keeps evaporating with little water coming in to take its place.

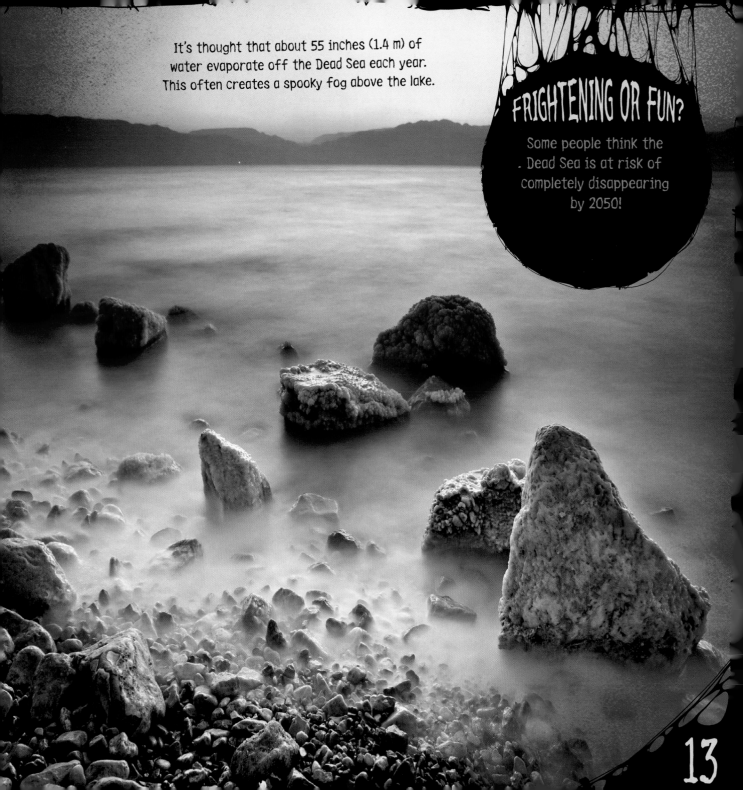

It's thought that about 55 inches (1.4 m) of water evaporate off the Dead Sea each year. This often creates a spooky fog above the lake.

13

SINKHOLES

The disappearing waters of the Dead Sea have a surprising—and scary—side effect. **Sinkholes** are forming when underground salt layers are broken down by freshwater. An increasing number of sinkholes are opening up as the waters of the lake withdraw more and more. No one knows where or when a sinkhole may open.

As of 2013, more than 3,000 sinkholes have been counted, compared to just 40 in 1990. They're dangerous. People have been hurt when the ground beneath them gave way!

Many areas around the Dead Sea are fenced off so people don't get hurt falling into sinkholes.

15

WHY WE CARE

Many animals call the **wetlands** around the Dead Sea home. Millions of birds use them as a place to have families. Some animals there are already in danger of dying out, such as the Arabian leopard. As the Dead Sea disappears, these creatures are in even more danger.

In 2013, a plan was approved to build a **canal** that would connect the Dead Sea and the Red Sea. This will bring freshwater to Jordan and Israel. However, some scientists worry the water will change the Dead Sea too much.

FRIGHTENING OR FUN?

Barbary falcons are one kind of bird that lives near the Dead Sea. They hunt other birds, even very fast ones!

Mediterranean Sea

Dead Sea

Canal

Nile River

Red Sea

A canal to bring water to the area around the Dead Sea would supply much-needed freshwater, but it would have unknown effects on the Dead Sea and its surrounding areas.

17

DEAD SEA SCROLLS

Between 1947 and 1956, people discovered something amazing in caves located near the northwestern shores of the Dead Sea. They found 800 **scrolls** made of animal skin, copper, and **papyrus**. The scrolls dated back to between 250 BC and 68 AD! They contained prayers, songs, and other texts.

No one knows for sure who wrote what are now called the Dead Sea Scrolls, but they're some of the oldest **religious** writings ever found. Historians study them to learn more about the Jewish and Christian religions.

The Dead Sea Scrolls, part of which is shown here, contain the oldest copy of the religious laws known as the Ten Commandments ever found.

VACATION PLACE

Despite its scary name, hundreds of thousands of people visit the Dead Sea each year. The Dead Sea offers them experiences they couldn't get at any other lake. Many people enjoy the area's rich history. Some believe the water has healing qualities. Others like to take mud baths there, while still others sit in the natural mineral springs.

Would you like to visit the Dead Sea? Let's hope the disappearing lake is still around for you to visit in the future!

FASCINATING FACTS ABOUT THE DEAD SEA

coast is lowest dry point on Earth

10 times saltier than the ocean

Dead Sea Scrolls were found in caves nearby

home to a new kind of bacteria

evaporating at a fast rate

normal aquatic life can't live there

more than 3,000 sinkholes have opened on its shores

contains more than 35 kinds of mineral salts

GLOSSARY

aquatic: living, growing, or spending time in water

bacteria: tiny creatures that can only be seen with a microscope

canal: a man-made waterway

evaporation: the process of changing from a liquid to a gas

Middle East: the area where southwestern Asia meets northeastern Africa

mineral: matter in the ground that forms rocks

papyrus: writing material made from the papyrus plant and used by ancient peoples

religious: having to do with a belief in and way of honoring a god or gods

saline: a liquid containing a high amount of salt

scroll: a roll of paper or other matter for writing a document

sinkhole: a hole in the ground that forms when rocks or soil are removed by flowing water

tributary: a river that joins a larger river or a lake

wetland: an area where the soil is soaked or covered with water

FOR MORE INFORMATION

Books

Burnham, Brad. *Qumran Caves: Hiding Place for the Dead Sea Scrolls.* New York, NY: PowerKids Press, 2003.

Furstinger, Nancy. *Jerusalem.* Edina, MN: ABDO Publishing, 2005.

Websites

The Dead Sea Scrolls
www.socialstudiesforkids.com/articles/religions/deadseascrolls.htm
Learn more about the Dead Sea Scrolls.

Is the Dead Sea Really Dead?
geography.howstuffworks.com/oceans-and-seas/dead-sea-dead.htm
Find out more fascinating facts about this body of water.

10 Things You Didn't Know About the Dead Sea
twistedsifter.com/2012/06/10-things-you-didnt-know-about-the-dead-sea/
Read the facts, and check out some awesome photographs.

INDEX